Largs – *Then & Now*

By Hugh Maxwell

Introduction

Largs occupies a sheltered position on a gently sweeping bay overlooking the Isle of Great Cumbrae. The town's name is derived from the Scots-Irish 'Learg' signifying a 'plain' and this describes perfectly the low-lying ground it occupies adjacent the Gogo Water which spills out into the Firth of Clyde.

It was the shelter of this gently-sloping ground on the coast which attracted the first settlers and evidence can be found in the area dating back to the Neolithic era when a tomb was discovered in the vicinity of Douglas Park. On nearby Knock Hill are the visible remains of a prehistoric hill fort whilst further east near Outerwards Farm are the remains of a Roman fortlet. Both locations were strategically important as they command excellent views over the surrounding district.

The Battle of Largs took place on the 2 October 1263 when the Viking king, Haakon, and his fleet ventured into the Firth of Clyde. The Vikings already controlled much of the northern and western seaboard and sought to strengthen their influence but the naval excursion was doomed as a fierce storm hit the fleet whilst at anchor in the waters off the Ayrshire coast. Many of the longships sank whilst others were driven ashore onto the rocks where the Scots, led by Alexander III, ruthlessly seized their opportunity and showed no mercy. The defeat diminished Viking influence and was an important event in shaping the future of Scotland and its people. In 1912 a monument was unveiled to commemorate the battle in the form of a tall Celtic round tower known locally as 'the Pencil'. It was built on the edge of the rocky shore, just to the south of the present town, overlooking the Firth of Clyde in the area known as the Bowen Craig.

In the twelfth century King Malcolm IV appointed Sir Richard Morville Great Constable of Scotland and also Lord of Cuninghame, Largs and Lauderdale. In feudal times, as royal authority spread throughout the south west of Scotland, Largs, which had always been a separate barony, was later amalgamated into the Cunninghame district.

The lordship of Largs eventually fell to the Stewarts and during the early fourteenth century a chapel, dedicated to St Columba and granted to the Monastery of Paisley, was built just north of the Gogo Water on a flat site near the shore. It was surrounding this kirk that the first houses and streets appeared of the present town and the oldest part of Largs is located here, just off Main Street, with its narrow quaint alleys and crooked lanes.

In 1595 Largs was granted a burgh charter through John Brisbane of Bishopton and by the seventeenth century had been formed into a parish. In 1750 the settlement became a burgh of barony and by 1800 Largs had its own turnpike road connecting it with the nearby towns of Saltcoats and Irvine.

Up until the nineteenth century Largs remained a typical coastal town on the Firth of Clyde, heavily dependant on fishing and weaving. In 1851 its population was only 2,824 and thirty years later this had only slightly increased to 3,079, but this was soon to change. A wooden pier had existed for many years but a longer stone pier was built in 1834 which allowed greater goods traffic and larger passenger steamers to travel down the Clyde from Glasgow. These vessels now visited Largs in ever increasing numbers and offered cruises to various resorts on the Clyde such as Arran,

Text © Hugh Maxwell, 2017.
First published in the United Kingdom, 2017,
by Stenlake Publishing Ltd.
Telephone: 01290 551122
www.stenlake.co.uk

ISBN 9781840337952

Printed by:
P2D, 1 Newlands Road, Westoning, MK45 5LD

**The publishers regret that they cannot supply
copies of any pictures featured in this book.**

Acknowledgements

The author would like to thank the people of Largs who willingly contributed information towards this book and also friends and family for their generous encouragement, support and assistance, in particular Jonathan who helped with the photography.

Further Reading

The Statistical Account of Scotland, 1791–1799.
The New Statistical Account of Scotland, 1845.
The Third Statistical Account of Scotland, 1951.
John Strawhorn, *Ayrshire – The Story of a County*, 1975.
Ken Andrew, *Ayrshire Guide*, 1981.
Andrew Miller Brown, *Largs and District in Old Picture Postcards*, 1987.
R. & M. McSherry, *Old Largs*, Stenlake Publishing, 1997.
Dane Love, *Ayrshire – Discovering a County*, 2003.
Alan Godfrey, *Old Ordnance Survey Maps, Largs 1895*, 2008.

Rothesay and Millport. Crowded paddle and turbine steamers became a regular sight at the pier and as a direct result the town began to prosper.

Many large villas and mansion houses were built by notable people and wealthy businessmen from Glasgow and John Street, Charles Street and Nelson Street all came into existence around this time. Handsome hotels, elaborate guest houses, cafes and shops were all established along Main Street, in the Broomfields and along the Gallowgate and Barrfield areas to cater for the visitors and in 1876 Largs became a Police Burgh. The railway was also eventually extended north from Fairlie to Largs in 1885 by the Glasgow and South Western Railway, making the town even more accessible. By the early 1900s the population had increased to just over 5,000.

The First World War saw the safe and sheltered anchorage of the bay widely used by the Royal Navy for its battleships and Clyde College was also used as a convalescent home for wounded soldiers. Largs popularity as a seaside resort peaked in the 1930s when it had 25 large hotels and at least an equal number of boarding and private guest houses. It was during this period that the burgh council constructed the bathing pavilion and changing rooms along the Victoria Esplanade whilst the Moorings Café and Dance Hall was also built near the pier head. Nardini's also chose to expand their popular ice cream business from Paisley and built a café facing directly onto the shore near Auchinhean. The large villa of Millburn was demolished to make way for the Viking Cinema, the train station was redesigned and an attractive pavilion was also built in the Barrfields as a variety theatre where many entertainers performed to crowds of over a thousand.

The outbreak of the Second World War changed things dramatically. Largs was to play an important role as the Hollywood Hotel in Greenock Road was requisitioned by the Royal Navy and became HMS Warren, the headquarters of Combined Operations. Known as the "Field of the Cloth of Gold" because of the number of high-ranking officers in attendance, a conference was held there in 1943 where it was decided that Normandy would be the location for the invasion of Europe.

The Barrfields Pavilion was requisitioned, becoming a maintenance depot and administrative centre for a squadron of flying boats or sea planes that were based in the Largs Channel. The patrol boats were Catalinas and Coronados and they could often be seen parked on the Barrfield putting greens in various states of repair whilst undergoing maintenance. Brisbane House, the long time home of the Brisbane family, was also demolished during the war when it was being used by commandos during training exercises. The end of hostilities saw a total of 67 names added to the war memorial on the seafront in front of the Sandringham building.

By 1951 the population had increased to around 8,500 and this would always increase at least threefold during the summer. Largs prospered and continued to be a popular destination on the west coast but by the early 1970s low cost package holidays were luring Glaswegians away from their traditional resorts. This saw the town decline in popularity as a holiday destination but nonetheless by the mid 1970s the population had increased to around 10,000.

In 1975 Largs was incorporated into Cunninghame District. The following years proved to be difficult as the town gradually adjusted to fewer holidaymakers but increasing numbers of day trippers. The loss of overnight trade during the summer months resulted in the closure of many hotels, guesthouses and giftshops.

Largs was now a town in transition and many boarded-up hotels were eventually demolished and replaced with modern housing and private flats for the increasing numbers of older people who were choosing to retire and live by the coast. Today, the town has continued to expand and adapt and a number of modern housing schemes have been created for the increasing number of families who have chosen to stay near the coast. Most residents now commute to find work in nearby towns although there are still a large number of inhabitants who are employed in the local cafes, shops, restaurants and hotels. The population now stands at around 11,250.

Largs Pier in 1908 with a crowded paddle steamer arriving to drop off and pick up passengers. Many steam packets operated from the pier at this time and they included the *St Mungo*, the *Victor*, the *Nimrod* and the *James Denniston*. They called regularly to Ardrossan and Ayr, Greenock and Glasgow as well as to Millport on a daily basis. Today the pier is still used regularly during the summer months by the PS *Waverley*, the last seagoing passenger-carrying paddle steamer in the world.

Storm damage at the pier on 29 November 1912. The small ticket office building was badly damaged with a large part of the wall ready to collapse into the sea. The view is from the pier into Main Street and the large amount of debris and rocks strewn around the streets shows how powerful the waves and wind must have been. A new ticket office and waiting room was later constructed just out of view to the left at the pierhead. Today the ticket offices and waiting room of Caledonian MacBrayne Ltd for the Largs to Millport ferry now occupy the site of the old ticket office and harbour master's building in the foreground of this view.

Main Street in 1911 with many people gathered near the pierhead. On the right at the corner of Bath Street is the frontage for Houston, the licensed grocer, while across the junction is Robert Orr & Son's grocer's shop which sold goods such as mild cured hams, Wiltshire smoked bacon, the finest Danish and Irish butter, fine old Dolro port and special old Highland whisky. Next door on Bath Street was the Royal Bank of Scotland.

The ticket offices and waiting rooms of the Glasgow & South Western Railway and Caledonian Steam Packet Company at the pierhead. Prior to the railway being extended to the town from Fairlie in 1885, the pierhead was where the horse drawn charabancs and carriages would queue, patiently waiting to take passengers on and off the many steamers that called on their excursions in the Firth of Clyde. It later became the bus terminus for Clyde Coast Services, linking with the ferry crossing to Cumbrae until the 1950s when it became too congested and was moved to another location just off Main Street. The ticket offices were demolished and replaced by a large amusements arcade that was built in 1955.

The tiled façade of Ye Olde Anchor Inn at 36 Gallowgate Street. Above the door can be seen the name of D. Haddow, the proprietor, who is possibly standing in the doorway.

Looking across the Gallowgate in the early 1900s towards Gallowgate Square, with the narrow Gallowgate Lane visible on the left. This is one of the oldest areas of the town and would have been the place for locals to witness guilty delinquents, bound by chains, being led up the Gallowgate Lane to nearby Green Hill and the waiting gallows. Visible in the square, surrounded by children, is the old Largs water pump dating from 1801. This was replaced in 1910 and then again in 1993 with an attractive stone well.

Looking northwards along Victoria Esplanade towards the Gallowgate in September 1926. Dominating the view is the spire of St Columba's Parish Church with the Royal Hotel adjacent, followed by the Victoria Hotel and then the gable of the Largs Hotel on the corner of Gallowgate Square. These hotels have long since closed although the buildings themselves have changed little.

Looking north along Victoria Esplanade in the early 1900s with many people gathered around the boat hirers. An extract from the *New Statistical Account of Scotland* of 1845 describes the great appeal of the town: 'Largs has long been in high repute as a watering-place. From the end of May till the middle of October, there is an additional population, varying from 300 or 400 to upwards of 1,000. Few places afford greater facilities for sea-bathing, it being easily practicable to bathe at all times of the tide, and to obtain a proper depth by wading a few yards. The whole coast is perfectly safe. The sea-breezes are of a peculiarly bracing and invigorating character and their salutary effects evident on crowds of annual visitors from the densely peopled towns of the interior.' This scene has changed greatly with the building of an arcade, restaurant and large car park.

Looking eastwards along Seamore Street around 1914. The attractive red sandstone terraced houses were built around 1910 and were unusual in that they were erected in an elliptical style surrounding a small garden visible in the centre of this photograph. There has been little change to this scene with only the removal of the metal railings and the wall surrounding the gardens.

Holidaymakers gather at the busy pierhead area at the top of Main Street in 1936 with The Moorings cafe visible on the right. It was built in 1935 to the designs of James Houston for the prominent Castlevecchi family, and is remembered with great fondness by many people who spent their holidays at Largs. Designed using a nautical theme, the cafe was a popular venue for lunches and teas and also had a restaurant and dance floor at the top. It was demolished and replaced in 1990 with a new building, also called The Moorings, which contains shops and flats.

This photograph taken during severe flooding on 17 January 1934 shows the shops at the top of Main Street, next to the pierhead, under deep water. Two local men can be seen travelling past in a canoe with Bruno Belli sitting in the front whilst 'Baldy' Brown is doing the rowing. Such was the ferocity of the storm and flood waters that towering waves which had been thrown onto the shore front were unable to recede quickly due to the power of the storm, a high tide and both the Gogo Water and Moors Burn also being in spate. Considerable flood damage was done to many of the properties near the top of Main Street, along the Gallowgate and into Nelson Street, and also into Bath Street. Today the Clydesdale Bank now occupies the prominent corner position adjacent the pierhead.

Looking west along Main Street towards the pierhead in the early 1900s. On the right is one of the three-storey sandstone tenements that were built near the turn of the century to replace some of the original single-storey thatched cottages that lined the principal street. The post office was located here at the corner of Bellman's Close; also visible is the gable advertising for the licensed grocer's shop run by F.J. Thomson with J. Robertson also advertising carriage hire – in later years his motor garage was located down the narrow lane.

Looking east along Main Street in 1910 with the post office visible on the left next to the narrow lane that was once known as Kirk Close (now Bellman's Close). The photographer is looking directly down another narrow lane, known as Tron Place, while Main Street can be seen winding its way round to the right past the train station just out of view.

The railway reached Largs on 1 June 1885 after the line was extended by the Glasgow and South Western Railway from Fairlie. Prior to this, travellers had to catch a charabanc or stagecoach at Fairlie, some three miles south, to reach the town and often their final stop would be the terminus at the pierhead. Surrounded by a glazed canopy, the new station was very elegant with four platforms spanned by a large metal footbridge on Gogo Street. A small goods station was also built which was accessed by carriers from near the Upper Gogo Bridge and a small turntable was located behind Hill Street. On 11 July 1995 a passenger train arriving from Glasgow Central failed to stop and crashed through the buffers, demolishing the ticket office, two shops and a large part of the station building before coming to a stop at the taxi rank on Main Street. Five people were injured. A new ticket office was built in 2001 and a new station building was completed in 2005.

A photograph of Largs Station in the early 1900s, taken from the metal passenger footbridge on Gogo Street, with four trains visible at the platforms. This was one of the busiest places in the town and a glazed canopy protected passengers from the worst of the elements. The line was constructed with two tracks and provided a direct link via Ardrossan to Glasgow which allowed holidaymakers to travel down to the coast during the summer months. Following the accident on the morning of 11 July 1995, when a train failed to stop and ploughed through the buffers, destroying most of the station, much of the grandeur was lost. Only two platforms now remain in use with a small ticket office being built in 2001, followed by a new smaller station building in 2005. Only two rail tracks are now in use, with those on the right hand side having been removed and converted into a small garden. The line southwards from the station to Ardrossan has also been reduced to a single track.

Looking north from the Irvine Road over the Upper Gogo Bridge and into Main Street around 1910. On the left men can be seen standing next to the entrance of the goods station operated by the Glasgow and South Western Railway. Construction work is underway to repair and widen the bridge. The three-storey Spencer Buildings, built in 1897, stand on Gogo Street overlooking the bridge while in the background is the towering chimney of the gas works, established in 1838 at Fraser's Close. The gas works was established through a share trust and first lit the houses, principal streets and parish church in 1839. Below the chimney, at the corner of Waterside Street, is the Burns' Tavern with its large portrait of Robert Burns visible above the entrance door; in 1911 the proprietor or 'spirit dealer' was Robert Mackie. The building on the right at the bridge is the burgh stores.

Looking towards Bath Street and the junction of Union Street from the South Esplanade in 1910. On the far left is the round gable of the Bath Hall which dates from 1816 and gave its name to the street. Excavations in the town have discovered remains of a Roman bath house. This area became known as the Alexandra Esplanade after King Edward VII's wife and visible in the middle of this view is St John's Free Church, built in 1886, followed on the right by the towering spire of Clark's Memorial Church, built in 1892. The elegant Victorian shelter on the right has since sadly been removed.

GREEN SHUTTERS TEAROOM, LARGS. 2035.

The Green Shutters Tearoom is located at the corner of Fort Street and Bath Street and is joined onto the former Bath Hall which can be seen on the right of this view. This was originally the caretaker's house for the baths which were erected through public subscription at a cost of £2,000 in 1816. They had hot and cold running baths and also a spacious billiard room and well-stocked reading room. This photograph dates from around 12 September 1965 and also partially visible is the spire of Clark's Memorial Church on the left while located behind the tearoom is the spire of St John's Free Church. On the far right is the war memorial. The former baths have now closed and the building is now the Brisbane Centre, used for local community events including the Largs' Players Comedy Theatre. The Green Shutters Tearoom and restaurant with its distinctive green window shutters remains popular today.

Looking east along Union Street from the junction with Bath Street around 1909. The building on the right was once known as Seaview G.F.S. Home and was opened in 1888 by the YWCA as a holiday home for overworked young girls and women requiring rest and recuperation at the coast. The house was converted into private flats in 1966. On the left a man can be seen standing outside the doorway of the two-storey house that would become the Dunn Memorial Hall. A single-storey hall was built onto the present building to commemorate the life of D. Guthrie Dunn, son of John Dunn who was a successful tobacco merchant and partner in the Glasgow tobacco manufacturing company F. & J. Smith. He lived in nearby Knock Castle and was tragically killed in 1933 after falling overboard from his yacht during the return leg of a round-the-world voyage. The entire estate was left to Mrs Agnes Stevens who had been the housekeeper at Knock Castle for twenty years. In his memory the hall was gifted to the St John's congregation on 25 March 1936. It is still used regularly by the community.

Model Yacht Pond, Largs.   M. 215.

The Model Yacht Pond at the Broomfields was built by the council in the early 1900s at the Castle Brae. The water was only about a foot in depth to allow children to paddle in and rescue their sunken vessel and the pond covered roughly half an acre in size. Many local shops sold wooden model yachts to sail on it. Races and displays were also held regularly. The pond was eventually converted into a children's play park; however, model boats can still be seen nearby at the Aubrey Crescent Pond which is used regularly by the Largs Model Boat Club, formed in 1996.

Looking north from the raised area known as the 'Lang Bank' at the Broomfields, September 1926. A large crowd is gathered in front of the Cadet Stand to watch one of the popular shows that were held for holidaymakers. Booked by the town council, troupes, pierrots, musicians and bands regularly performed two or three times a day. Originally the sloping ground in front of the stand was terraced to allow people to watch the entertainments but due to the often inclement weather covered seating was provided in front of the stage, as can be seen here. Today all trace of the pavilion has disappeared and a small skateboard park and ice cream kiosk now occupy the site.

Burnmouth Villa was located on the Greenock Road facing west onto the Noddsdale Green and Largs Bay. It took its name from the Moor Burn which flows down off the surrounding hills behind the house and tumbles past it, just to the right of this view, and into the sea. This scene was taken around 1912 and Burnmouth Villa was demolished in 1961, with the site now occupied by the St Mary's Star of the Sea Catholic church which was built the following year. All that remains today is the small wall on the right which surrounds the garden of the adjacent Moorburn House. Moor Burn can still be seen flowing under the modern concrete promenade and into the sea.

The Curling Hall was built on The Crescent at the Broomfields in 1813 by retired surgeon Dr John Cairnie, who became founder and president of the Royal Caledonian Curling Club in 1838. Following his death, the Curling Hall was bought by John Clark, provost of Largs from 1883 to 1889, and he built two large extensions onto each side of the original building. It later became the Curlinghall Hotel and in 1957 an extension was built joining it onto the adjacent Marine Hotel. It was thereafter known as the Marine and Curlinghall Hotel. Many locals will still remember the hotel's ballroom that could accommodate over 600 people at the regular Saturday night dances and also the Bruce lounge and cocktail bar. The hotel was demolished in 1983 and flats now occupy the site, but the name is remembered in the small cul-de-sac that was created called Curlinghall.